The Birth of a

by Barbara Wood

Illustrations by Jeff Nishinaka

HAMPTON-BROWN

Where do islands come from? How do they get in the middle of the ocean? Some islands start as volcanoes!

▲ Krakatoa Island

▲ Stromboli Island

The bottom of the ocean looks quiet. It is not.
Something is happening.

ocean floor

There is a crack in the ocean floor. Hot, melted rock pushes through the crack. The melted rock is called magma.

magma

The volcano erupts. The magma flows out. Now it is called lava. The lava gets hard. More lava flows out. It gets hard. The volcano starts to look like a mountain under the water.

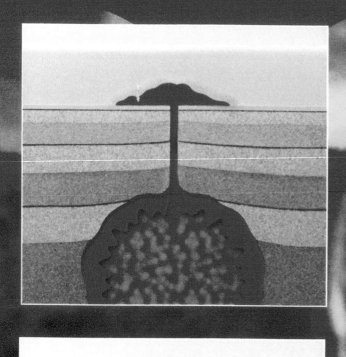

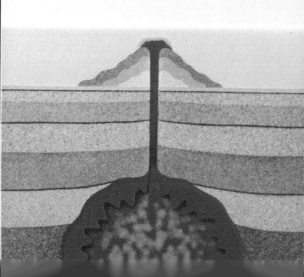

The volcano heats the water. The water boils. Steam rises.

▲ This steam rose in January of 2001.
   The volcano became the island of Kavachi.

The volcano grows taller and taller. Finally, the volcano is above the water! Now it is an island.

The volcano erupts again and again. The island grows bigger and bigger.

Then the volcano is quiet. It does not erupt.
Hundreds of years pass. Plants and trees grow.

Birds and other animals come to live on the island.

Plants

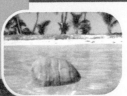

Seeds float on the water.

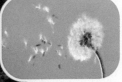

The wind carries seeds.

Ships carry seeds.

Animals

Birds and insects fly to the island.

Ships bring animals.

Some animals swim.

The island gets older. Strong winds blow away
sand and soil.

Waves crash against rocks. The waves carry tiny bits of rock away. The island starts to fall into the sea.

Then one day the ground begins to shake. Steam comes from the volcano. Magma pushes to the top.

The volcano erupts! Ashes and rocks burst into the air. Lava flows out. Trees burn.

▲ Hot lava can be very dangerous. Some lava moves faster than a car!

The lava gets hard. The sky clears.
The island is growing again!